The Secret Life Of Cats

by Sam Hogan
Illustrated by Leo Antolini

OXFORD
UNIVERSITY PRESS

Sleep

Many cats like to curl up on a comfortable chair and sleep. In fact, cats can sleep for over 14 hours a day! However, when they <u>finally</u> wake up, they like to play and explore.

<u>Finally</u> means after a long time. What do you think this cat will do now he has <u>finally</u> woken up?

pat pat

Playtime!

Cats like to play chasing and jumping games. If they see a ball, they like to jump <u>forwards</u> and tap it with their paws. They also play with balls of wool. When the wool unwinds, it looks a bit like a mouse's tail!

Show me how you might spring <u>forwards</u> like a cat.

tap
tap

Adventure Time!

Cats like to explore the outdoors. Some cats don't even need their owners to let them in and out – they can <u>enter</u> and exit their home using a cat flap.

Sometimes there might be a high fence or wall blocking the cat's path. It can't go forwards, but it can go upwards instead! A cat can jump six times its own height.

tap tap

Look at the picture of the cat flap. Do you think a person could use it to <u>enter</u> a building?

Acrobats

Cats have amazing balance. They know <u>exactly</u> where to put their feet so that they can walk along the top of a narrow fence. Cats use their tails to help them balance. Even if they fall, cats almost always land on their feet!

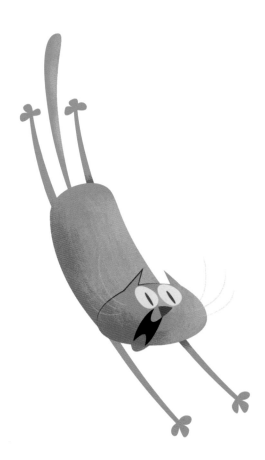

The word 'exactly' shows that the cat knows *just* where to put its feet. What might happen if the cat didn't put its feet down <u>exactly</u> in the correct place?

child

tap tap tap

9

Meeting Another Cat

Pet cats like to be by themselves. If they meet another cat, it can make them stressed and unhappy. They might hiss at each other. Finally, if neither cat backs down, they might fight!

Think About the Book

What do cats do?

101 WAYS TO BEAT BOREDOM

ANNA CLAYBOURNE

CONTENTS

BORED?

There's nothing on TV ...

Did you know that you'll probably spend a third of your life asleep? And you'll spend over 2660 days in school. Wow! That's a lot of time. So your free time is *really* important. Don't waste it being bored!

So how can you make the most of your time? Simple. All you need are some ideas. 101 to be exact! Now, 101 things might sound like a lot. But don't worry – you don't have to do everything. In fact, you don't even need to read this book from start to finish. You can start in the middle! Go on. Have a look and if you're feeling brave, take your first challenge.

I'm BORED. What can I do?

1

Fun for your friends

We think there is an activity in here for everybody. Can you find one for each of your friends?

PUT ON A PLAY

Do you want to be an actor one day? Why not start now? Get your friends together and put on a play. Parents, pals and pets can be the audience!

A play is really quite simple. All you need is:

- a story
- dialogue (what people say)
- actions (what people do).

How about retelling a story you know? Choose your favourite book or film and turn it into a play.

The Creepwood Mystery

Scene 1

Lord Sneer: Welcome to Creepwood Castle, my dear!

Emily: Thank you. My sister Gertie should be here any minute ...

[a knock at the door]

Lord Sneer: Who's that?

Emily: Gertie?

Top Tip!
Start a new line each time a different character speaks.

3 Set the stage

Use cardboard, paper or even an old bed sheet to make a painted **backdrop**.

4 Dress up

Make costumes for your characters using old clothes or scrap material.

5 Make a poster

Include a big picture and the names of all the stars!

6 Make it real

Make a play about something that really happened to you.

7 New adventures

Think of your favourite TV character. Can you make a play about them?

8 Big number

Add a song and dance routine to your play.

9 Curtain call

For the finishing touch, use a sheet to make a stage curtain.

Top Tip!
Use lots of actions and funny voices in your play.

If you have a spy in your play, why not try ideas 71 to 76?

10 AMAZE YOUR FRIENDS!

Tell your friends you can step through a postcard. They don't believe you? Then do it before their very eyes!

Wish You Were Here!

1. Take a normal, boring postcard that no one wants.

2. Fold the card in half lengthways.

4. Carefully cut along the fold from point A to point B.

A

B

3. Then cut lines in the card as in this diagram.

5. Carefully open up the card into a big loop, and step through it. Ta-daaa!

11 Curious coin

Take a large coin. Fix the coin between the teeth of two forks. Balance the coin on the edge of a glass. Magic!

12 Cracker challenge

Challenge your friends to eat three crackers in three minutes. No water allowed!

13 Paper fold puzzle

How many times can you keep folding a piece of paper in half?

14 Mysterious Mobius strip

Take a strip of paper. Twist one end over, then stick the two ends together to make a loop. Cut down the length of the strip. What happens?

15 Floating hands

Stand in a doorway and press the backs of your hands hard against the frame for one minute. When you step out, your hands will have a mind of their own!

16 Balancing act

Stand on one foot, then close your eyes. Count to 10. Do you start to fall over?

17 What a hoot!

Cup your hands together. Leave a gap between your thumbs. Blow across it at the right angle to make an owl sound.

SNAIL RACING

Ever wondered how quickly a snail moves? Now's your chance to find out!

1. On a piece of cardboard, draw three circles.
2. Collect a snail each.
3. Put stickers on their shells to show whose is whose.
4. Put them in the middle of the smallest circle.
5. See whose snail reaches the big circle first.

You will need:
- cardboard
- crayons
- stickers

Top Tip!
Be nice to your snails and put them back where you found them!

19 **Make your own board game**

Design a game board on cardboard, and use coins or tiny toys for counters.

20 **Need dice?**

Write the numbers 1 to 6 on pieces of card and put them in a bag. To 'roll' the dice, pick one out.

21 **Flying welly**

Take turns to fling a welly as far as you can outside. Measure your score in footsteps.

22 **The human knot**

Stand in a ring of 6 to 16 people. Put your right hand in the middle. Hold onto another person's right hand. Do the same again with your left hand. Without letting go, try to untangle the knot.

23 **Keepy-uppy**

Pass a ball between friends. How long can you go before dropping it?

24 **Tantalising target**

Try throwing balls into a plastic bucket. It's the simplest game ever, but we bet you'll still be doing it at bedtime!

25 **The IF game**

Ask your friends 'What would you do if ... ?' questions to find out more about them!

26 MAKE A PAPER BOAT

When can paper float?
When it's your very own paper boat!

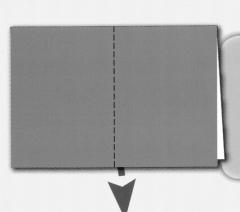

1. Fold a rectangular piece of paper in half lengthways, then open up and fold widthways.

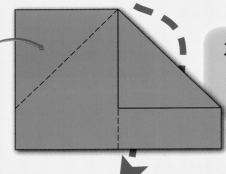

2. Fold the top corners over to the middle line.

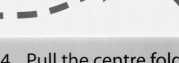

3. Fold up the two flaps at the bottom one to each side.

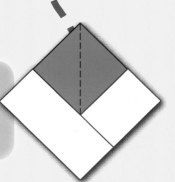

4. Pull the centre folds out and press flat into a diamond shape.

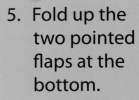

5. Fold up the two pointed flaps at the bottom.

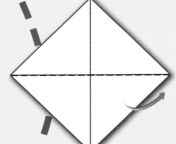

6. Again, pull the centre folds out and press flat to make a diamond.

27 The great boat race

Blow your paper boats along a tray of water using straws. Who can reach the other side first?

28 Create a rainbow

With your back to the Sun, spray a garden hose. A rainbow should appear in the spray!

29 Daredevil diver

Hold a ruler on the edge of a bath. Stand a toy figure on the end outside the bath. Press down on the other end of the ruler. Boinngg! Your diver will leap into the water.

30 Pooh sticks

You need a bridge over a stream. On the count of three, each person drops a stick into the water. See whose floats out the other side first.

31 Clean race

Have a car wash challenge. See who can finish first – or whose bit is shiniest!

32 Water fight

Split into two teams. Then try to get each other as wet as possible! Make sure you are outside!

Top Tip!

See if your boat floats – try it out in the bath!

7. Pull the top folds outwards and flatten the sides. There's your boat!

Your finished boat is ready to set sail.

NATURE HUNT

How well do you know the area you live in?
Take the Nature Hunt challenge and see
what you can discover.

You can do this in your garden or a local park.
Copy the table and see how much you can find.

Can you spot ...	Draw/write what you see
six different-shaped leaves	oak leaf
five different seeds	
four different kinds of birds	robin blackbird
three different flowers	
two creepy-crawlies (insects, spiders, slugs or snails)	
one animal's home	bird's nest

34 Make your own

You don't need to stick to our nature hunt. Write your own to suit the season and the place you live in.

35 Catch a spider's web

Tie three twigs together in a triangle. Stand it outside. After a few days, check to see if a spider has set up home!

36 Make it grow

Collect seeds from fruit. Plant them in a pot and see if they grow. Remember to water them!

37 The longest daisy chain ever!

Pick a daisy and use your thumbnail to make a hole in the stalk. Slip another daisy through, and keep going!

38 Spot it

Make sketches in a notebook of the things you spot. Note where and when you saw them.

39 Skimming stones on water

Hold a flat stone with your **index finger** against one edge. Flick the stone as you throw. It should bounce over the water!

Be good to your friends – throw a party!
Be good to your mum and dad – help
do the cooking!

How to Make the Perfect Pizza

You will need:

3 cups of flour
1/2 tsp. salt
1 tsp. sugar
1 cup of warm water
1 tsp. dried yeast
1 tbsp. olive oil
Your favourite toppings

- Put the dry ingredients in a bowl.
- Add the water and olive oil.
- Mix it into a ball.
- **Knead** the dough, then leave it for 1 hour.
- Roll out the dough into a pizza shape.
- Add tomato sauce, grated cheese and your favourite toppings.
- Get a grown-up to cook it for 20 minutes.

For party game ideas, see ideas 10 to 17 and 22.

Top Tip!
It's important to get the measurements right. Here's what they mean:

tsp. – teaspoon

tbsp. – tablespoon

41 **Dress fancy**

Think of a theme for your party. You could all dress like pirates!

42 **Get creative**

Design and send invitations to your friends. Don't forget the place, date, time and theme.

43 **Dress the room**

Make decorations to match your theme.

44 **Game on**

Make sure you prepare a few party games.

45 **Party punch**

Make **punch**. Mix equal parts tropical fruit juice, lemonade and fizzy water in a bowl. Add fruit.

46 **Tune up**

Put together songs or music to play.

47 **Yummy bugs!**

Make half a pack of jelly. When it is set, put creepy-crawly sweets on the jelly. Then make the rest of the jelly and pour on top.

48 GO STARGAZING

The next time it's a dark clear night – look up! In the sky you should see lots of beautiful stars. These stars make up shapes called constellations. Why not try to spot these three?

Orion

The **constellation** Orion is named after a hunter in Greek **myths**. Can you see the three stars in the middle that make his belt?

The Plough

Cassiopeia
(say ka-see-oh-pee-a)

16

52 Shadow shapes

Shine a torch at the wall in a dark room. Put your hands in front of it and see what animal shapes you can make.

49 Look north

Find the Plough and follow the two stars at the end of it upwards. There you'll find the North Star.

53 Moth-catching

In a garden, spread out a white sheet and shine a torch onto it. Moths will come to it and you can get a close look at them.

50 Make a wish

If you see a streak of light zoom across the sky, it's a shooting star. Don't forget to make a wish on it!

54 Spooky stories

On a dark night, tell each other your favourite spooky tales. Don't have nightmares!

51 Moon diary

Sketch how the Moon looks each night. How does it change?

55 Scary face

Shine a torch up at your face from under your chin. How scary can you look?

56 MOVING MONSTER

How do you catch a moving monster? By drawing it in a flipbook. Flick the pages and watch it come to life.

You will need:
- a small notepad with lots of pages
- a pencil or crayons

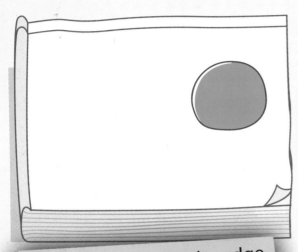

1. Draw a circle at the edge of the page.

2. Turn the page. Now draw the same circle but move it slightly. Repeat this two more times.

3. Turn the page. Now make your circle into a monster.

4. Turn the page. Draw the monster but with its arms up in the air.

Top Tip!
In order to make your monster move for longer, only make a small change each time.

5. Turn the page. Draw the monster with its arms back down.

6. Test it! Flick the pages and watch the monster move. Could you make your flip book better by making the changes on each page even smaller?

57 Flip more

Try making another flipbook. Can you make a baby monster hatch from an egg?

58 Never-ending story

Write four words of a story – "Once upon a time". Then pass it to a friend to write four more words. Keep passing on the story … it may never end!

59 Write to a writer

Write a letter to your favourite author. (Be polite!) You might even get a letter back.

60 Start a diary

Try to write down something funny, interesting or sad that happens to you each day.

61 Be a journalist

Start your own magazine. It could be about anything!

62 Swap it

Swap books with your friends. You might discover some great stories.

If you like to make a mess, this is for you! Try being a modern artist and make this picture.

You will need:

- empty yoghurt pots
- runny paint
- string

Get painting

1. Spread out *lots* of newspaper.
2. Place a big piece of plain paper on top of the newspaper.
3. Ask a grown-up to make a small hole in the bottom of each yoghurt pot.
4. Tie string around each pot. Leave 30 cm of string free.
5. Half-fill each yoghurt pot with a different colour of paint.
6. Now lift the pots by their strings and swing them over the paper.

You could even make your art into invitations for idea 42.

Top Tip!
Make sure you use lots of old newspaper and wear old clothes. This is really messy!

64 No paintbrushes
Try painting with different things like twigs, tissue paper or even your toes!

65 Take a line for a walk
Draw a picture without taking your pencil off the paper.

66 Doodle bug
Doodle over a piece of paper. Then fill in the shapes with different colours.

67 Art without eyes
Put on a blindfold. Can you draw a house, a person, a flower or a rocket?

68 No hands
Try making a picture by holding a pen between your toes.

69 What next?
Once your works of art are dry, make them into cards.

70 Steal their style
Find an artist you really like and try to copy their style.

This style of painting is known as abstract art.

SPY WRITING

Ever wondered how spies send secret messages? You can do it yourself – with invisible ink!

For your ink, use lemon juice. Spell out your message on a piece of paper using a small paintbrush. Wait for it to dry. Then it's ready to send.

To see the message, your fellow spies must leave it on a warm radiator, or in bright sunlight. The letters will turn brown and become readable.

Top Tip!
You can use apple juice or clear vinegar instead.

72 Keep it secret

Write down the alphabet and give each letter a different number. This is your code. Write your message in the code. Only someone with a copy of the code will be able to crack it.

73 Pass the word

All good spy clubs need a password. It should be a made-up word that no one will guess, like 'squirdlepip'.

74 Wrap it up

Wrap a strip of paper around a pen in a spiral. Write your message along it, then unwrap it. Your spy contacts can only read it by wrapping it around the same sized pen.

75 Guess who?

Spies often need a disguise. Wear dark glasses, a hat and even a fake moustache.

76 Speak gibberish

Drive your parents bonkers by speaking in code. Simply add a short code word to the middle of every syllable you say. Try cracking this code: Muogm's progeseognt iogs iogn mogy roogom.

77 BRRR-ILLIANT ICE SCULPTURE

When the weather's freezing cold, let nature make you an ice sculpture.

You will need:
- modelling dough
- leaves, pebbles, twigs
- ribbon or string
- water

1. Make a hollow mould out of modelling dough.

2. Then put leaves, pebbles and twigs in it.

3. Put the mould outside and carefully fill it with water.

4. Place a loop of ribbon in the top and leave it to freeze.

5. When it's solid, take off the modelling dough.

6. Hang up your sculpture outside.

Top Tip!
If it's not freezing, use the freezer instead.

78 Angel in the snow

Lie down in the snow. Open and shut your legs and flap your arms by your sides. Carefully stand up. There's an angel where you were lying!

79 Snow monsters

Never mind boring old snowmen! Can you make a three-headed alien or dragon out of snow? Don't forget to give your monster a cosy scarf.

80 Monster melt

Time how long your monsters take to melt. Whose lasts longest?

81 Catch snowflakes

Get a piece of black card or fabric and keep it in the freezer. When snow is falling, take it outside and catch a few snowflakes on it. Use a magnifying glass to get a good look.

82 Winter warmer

Brrrrr! After all that, you need to get warm. Mix three teaspoons of hot chocolate powder into a cup of warm milk. Top with squirty cream, mini marshmallows or chocolate flakes. Yum!

Too warm for snow monsters? Try idea 91 instead.

CORNFLOUR SLIME

Investigate the weird world of slime!
This isn't any ordinary slime though!
Make it and find out why.

You will need:
- 2 cups of **cornflour**
- a bowl
- water
- green food colouring

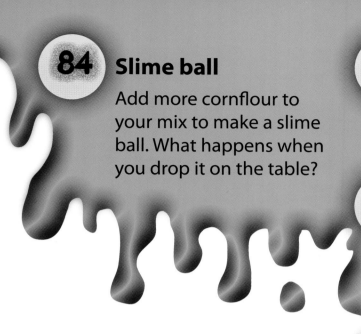

84 Slime ball

Add more cornflour to your mix to make a slime ball. What happens when you drop it on the table?

What to do

Put the cornflour in a bowl. Add water bit by bit until it's a gloopy mix. Add a little green food colouring to make it look like slime.

Now for the fun stuff! See what happens to the slime when you:

- stir the slime slowly
- stir the slime quickly
- hit the slime.

85 Does other slime do this?

What happens if you make slime using normal flour? Can you do the same tricks?

86 Defy gravity

Completely fill a paper cup with water. Lay a postcard on top. Turn them upside down. Now take your hand away. The postcard will stay!

87 Which is which?

How can you tell a boiled egg from a raw egg? Spin each egg then stop them. When you let go, the raw egg will start spinning again!

88 Taste test

Try tasting slivers of apple, raw onion and raw cabbage while holding your nose. Can you tell which is which?

89 Test your reaction time

Ask a friend to hold a ruler in the air. Hold your thumb and finger apart at the bottom of the ruler. Get your friend to drop the ruler. Measure where you caught the ruler.

90 Confuse your brain

Try moving your right foot **clockwise** while drawing a number six in the air with your right hand.

SAND ANIMALS

A day at the beach is brilliant fun. But once you've had a paddle and eaten your picnic, what can you do? Well, how about making sand animals?

Make a pile of sand and shape it into an animal. Try a dolphin, whale, snake, turtle or a curled-up cat.

Top Tip!
Use sand that's a bit damp for the best sand sculptures.

Sand sculptures can be small like this turtle or large like this one in Belgium.

92 World's biggest!

The biggest sandcastle ever made was over 9 m tall! Yours probably won't be that big but make the biggest, most beautiful castle you can.

93 X marks the spot

Make a map of an imaginary island in the sand. You could even bury some treasure!

94 Monster feet

Use sand to give someone enormous feet, with huge warty toes. (Shells make good warts.)

95 Pile the pebbles

Make a balancing tower of beach pebbles. How tall can you make it?

96 Fly a kite

Two twigs, a plastic bag, sticky tape and string can make a perfect kite.

97 Rock-pooling

What creatures are lurking in the rock pools? Look closely under stones and among the seaweed.

98 Beachcombing

Search for treasure! You might find seashells, **sea glass**, or precious stones like **jet** and **amber**.

99 Shrink your friends

Put a beach ball on the ground. Get a friend to stand about 30 steps away. Move your head so that their feet line up with the top of the ball. Take a photo. They will look tiny!

100 Flip-flop flinging

A summer version of welly throwing. See idea 21.

101

RELAX!

Phew! You must be worn out. It's great to have loads to do, but don't forget to take some time to rest.

Enjoy your free time. Before you know it, it will be time to go back to school – or time for bed! Sleep well.

GLOSSARY

amber yellow-orange-coloured precious stone

backdrop painted scenery at the back of a stage

clockwise in the direction the hands of a clock move

constellation pattern that seems to appear in the stars

cornflour fine flour made from corn (also called maize)

index finger finger you use for pointing

jet black precious stone

knead mix by pressing, folding and pulling

myth old, impossible or untrue story

punch party drink made by mixing lots of drinks together

sea glass small pieces of smooth glass found on beaches that has been smoothed by the water and sand

INDEX